W9-BUV-150

First edition for the United States and Canada published
in 2006 by Barron's Educational Series, Inc.

First edition for Great Britain published
in 2006 by Hodder Children's Books

All inquiries should be addressed to:
Barron's Educational Series, Inc.
250 Wireless Boulevard
Hauppauge, New York 11788
www.barronseduc.com

Library of Congress Control Number: 2005934216

ISBN-13: 978-0-7641-3215-5
ISBN-10: 0-7641-3215-6

Printed in China
9 8 7 6 5 4 3 2 1

Disclaimer
The Web site addresses (URLs) included in this book were
valid at the time of going to press. However, because of
the nature of the Internet, it is possible that some addresses
may have changed, or sites may have changed or closed
down since publication. While the publisher regrets any
inconvenience this may cause readers, no responsibility for
any such changes will be accepted by the publisher.

Do I Have to Go to the Hospital?

A FIRST LOOK AT GOING TO THE HOSPITAL

PAT THOMAS
ILLUSTRATED BY LESLEY HARKER

BARRON'S

It's not fun
being sick.

When you are sick you don't
feel much like playing or talking
or eating, so there's not a lot
to do.

Most of the time when you are hurt or ill you can get better at home. Your parents know a lot about how to take care of you.

They know how to bandage your knee, take your temperature, tuck you up nice and warm in bed, and give you lots of cuddles to help you feel better.

What about you?

What do your parents do to help you feel better when you are sick?

But sometimes when you are very sick it's best to have a doctor or a nurse help look after you.

This may mean a visit to the doctor's office or even to the hospital.

Sometimes your parents and your doctors plan for you to go to the hospital for special care.

But some visits to the hospital are not planned.

Some people need to stay in the hospital for only a few hours, but some people need to stay longer.

What about you?

Can you think of some reasons why people go to the hospital? Have you ever been to a hospital?

Going into the hospital can be scary. Hospitals are big, busy places. You may hear new noises, smell new smells, and see people getting all kinds of care.

There may be lots of people who you don't know and who don't know you.

That's why you will be given a special bracelet with your name on it. The doctors and nurses wear badges with their names, too.

The doctors and nurses in hospitals have gone to special schools to learn lots of ways of making you feel better.

Your parents trust them and you can, too.

What about you?

How do you feel about going to
the hospital? Are there any questions
you would like to ask?

At the hospital they have special machines that can take pictures of the inside of your body, or check what's in your blood.

They have tools for listening to your heartbeat and mending broken bones.

They also have special medicines to help you get better.

There may be other
children there, and you may
share a room with one or
more of them.

This means you will have someone to talk to and keep you company.

You can still do things like play games, read books,
and watch television while you are in the hospital.

And there will be a telephone so you can talk to your friends and family if you want to. Just because you are by yourself sometimes doesn't mean you have to feel alone.

Your parents will be able to stay at the hospital and you may also have visitors.

They can bring
you toys and books
and tell you all
about what is
happening at home.

Nobody likes going to the hospital.
But sometimes you really do
have to.

And because of all the special care you are getting, it won't be long before you are feeling better and are happy to be home.

HOW TO USE THIS BOOK

Hospitals can be undermining for parents and frightening for children. You can help make the experience more positive by making sure that your child is allowed to express feelings and ask questions. A child who is adequately prepared for what will happen in the hospital will find the adjustment much easier than one who is not. You know your child best and already have the skills to help. However, here are some things to consider:

This book focuses mostly on the emotional experience of going to the hospital rather than specific procedures. Whatever procedures your child needs, make sure you find a way to explain them in language that is simple and reassuring but not misleading. For instance, don't say something won't hurt when it will, don't promise a quick release from the hospital if your child needs an extended stay. If you don't know the answer to a specific question it is OK to say so. But also make a promise that you will find out more from the doctor.

Try to stay calm. Your child can pick up on your level of fear and be frightened by it. You can ease your own fears by asking questions beforehand about what will happen. It can help to make a list of questions to ask before any meeting with a doctor. If you don't understand the answer, ask the doctor to explain it to you again in a way you and your child can understand.

Allow your children to feel whatever they are feeling about going to the hospital. Don't judge them. Occasionally parents want their children to reassure *them* by "being good" about going into the hospital. As an adult, it is *your* job to do the reassuring. Instead of insisting on a positive attitude, find out what is behind the fear. It could be a lack of understanding of the condition, unanswered questions about procedures—especially if they involve surgery—scary stories other children have told them, a previous negative experience in the hospital, or even fear of dying. You'll never know unless you gently help your children to talk about it.

Play doctor with your children. Bandage a teddy bear's or doll's arm, put its foot in a pretend cast, or pretend to take a blood sample. All of these things will help familiarize your children with the kinds of procedures they may be exposed to in the hospital.

Schools can help familiarize children with the concept of hospitals by arranging visits from nurses and doctors in the local community who can talk to them about what hospitals are and what happens there. There is ample evidence that such visits can help children cope better should they eventually have to go to the hospital.

BOOKS TO READ

Clifford Visits the Hospital
by Norman Bridwell (Scholastic, 2000)

Franklin Goes to the Hospital
by Paulette Bourgeois and Brenda Clark
(Scholastic, 2000)

Going to the Doctor
by Anne Civardi (Usborne First Experiences, 2000)

Going to the Hospital
by Fred Rodgers and Jim Judkis
(PaperStar Books, 1997)

Good-Bye Tonsils!
by Juliana Lee Hatkoff, Craig Hatkoff, Marilyn
Mets (Viking Children's Books, 2001)

Let's Talk About When You Have to Have Your Tonsils Out
by Melanie Apel Gordon (PowerKids Press, 2000)

RESOURCES FOR ADULTS

American Academy of Pediatrics (AAP)
National Headquarters:
The American Academy of Pediatrics
141 Northwest Point Boulevard
Elk Grove Village, IL 60007-1098
847/434-4000
847/434-8000 (Fax)

Washington, DC Office:
The American Academy of Pediatrics
Department of Federal Affairs
601 13th Street, NW
Suite 400 North
Washington, DC 20005
202/347-8600
202/393-6137 (Fax)
www.aap.org
e-mail: *kidsdocs@aap.org*

American Academy of Pediatrics (AAP) is an organization of 60,000 pediatricians committed to the attainment of optimal physical, mental, and social health and well-being for all infants, children, adolescents and young adults. Their Web site provides quick access to a variety of children's health topics and a physician referral service.

KidSource OnLine
www.kidsource.com
In-depth and timely education and healthcare information that will make a difference in the lives of parents and children.